While this may be a cursive practice book I have endeavored to create something of stronger value by adding the advanced practice section.

The advanced section has excerpts of text for each entry that must be copied rather than traced.

The very end of the book also provides many resources to expand the learning further.

1
2
3
is for
Agate

3
1
2
4
B is for
Bloodstone

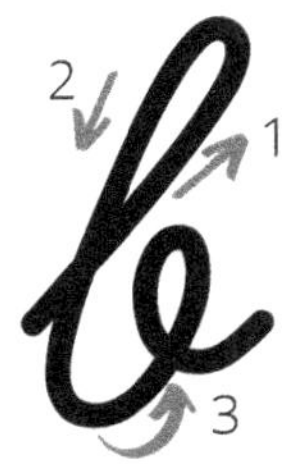

b b b b b b b b b b b b b b b b

b b b b b b b b b b b b b b b b b b b

b b b b b b b b b b b b b b b b b b b b

1
C
is for
Citrine

D is for Dichroite

1
2
3
4

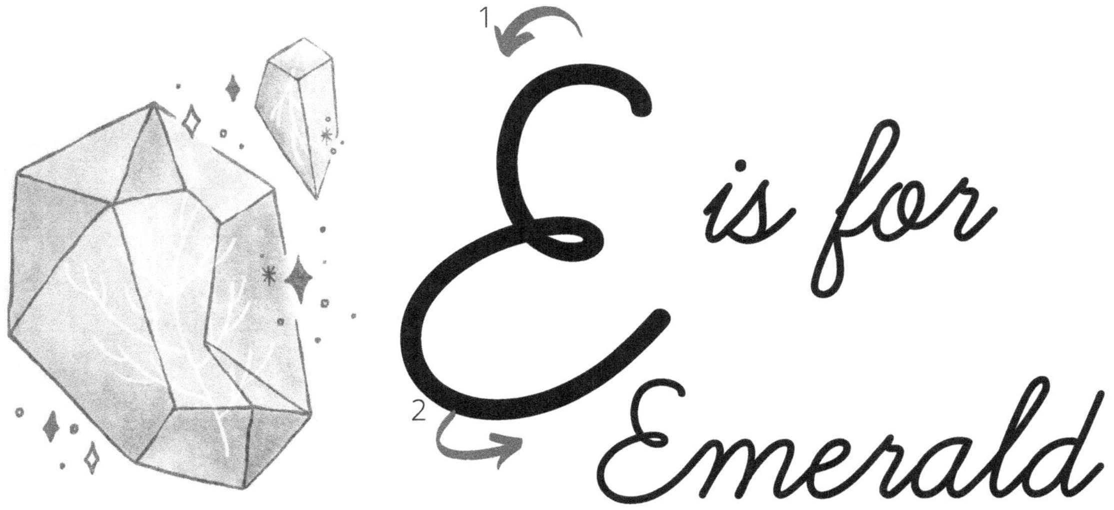

1
2
E is for
Emerald

$\mathscr{F}$ is for Fluorite

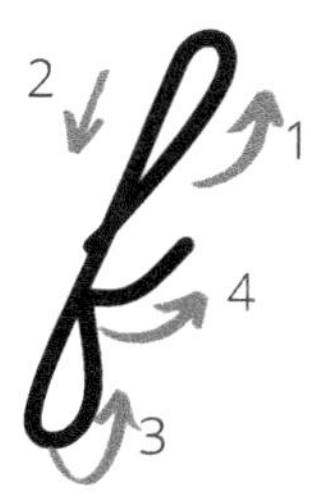

1
2
3
4
is for
Garnet

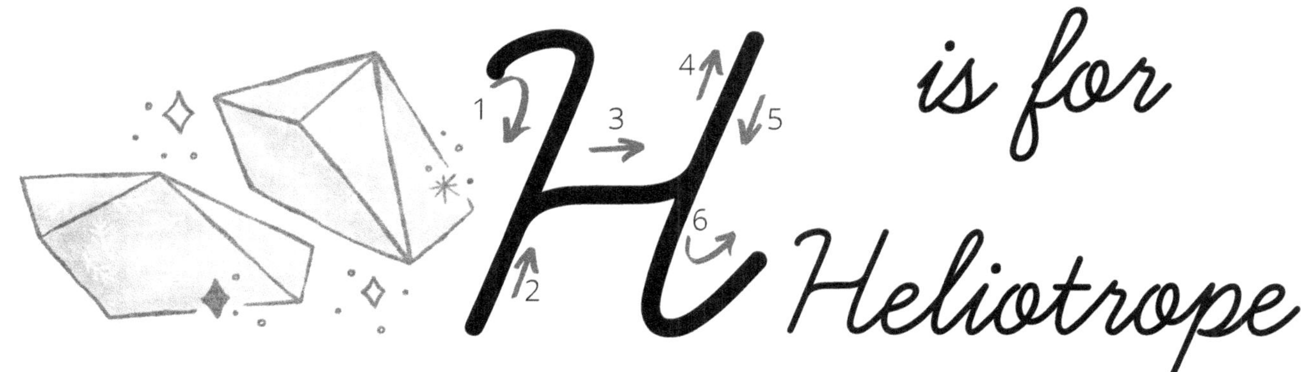

is for
Heliotrope

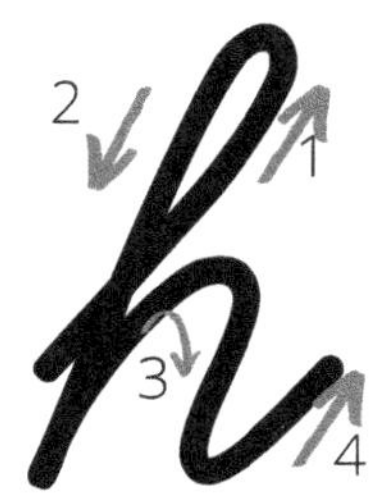

2
1
I is for
Indicolite

i

1
2
3
is for
Jade

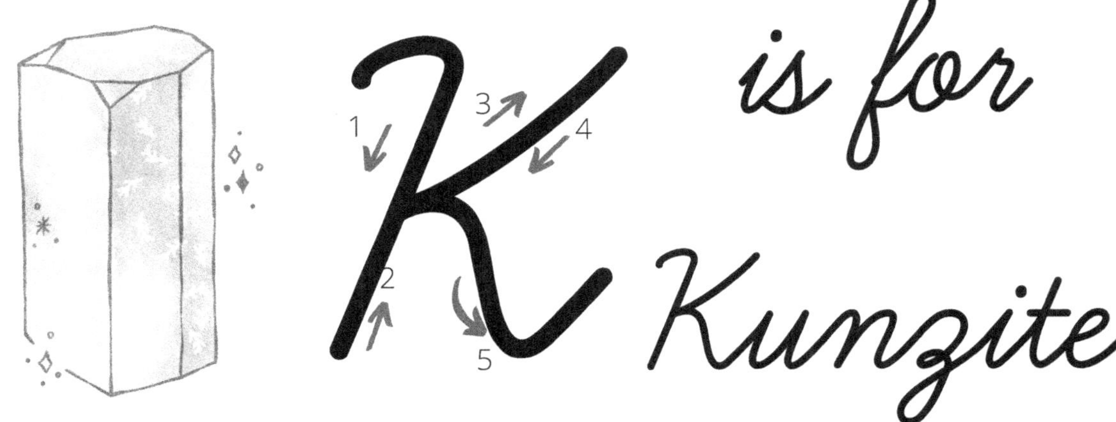

1
2
3
4
5
is for
Kunzite

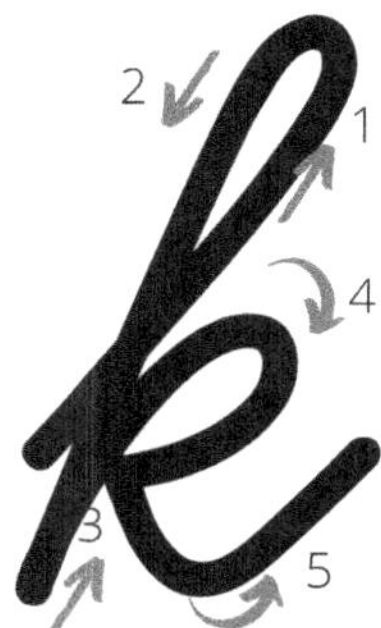

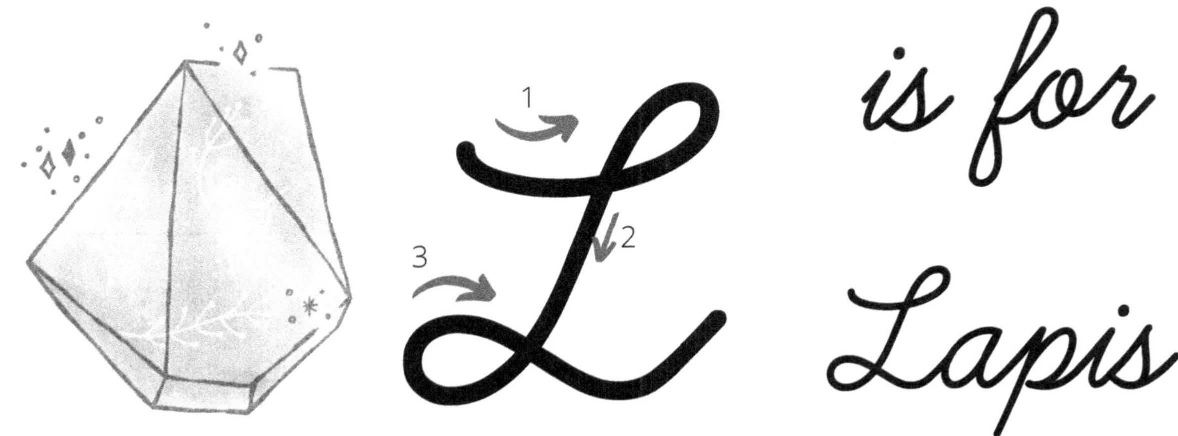

1
2
3
L
is for
Lapis

1
2
3
4
5
M
is for
Morganite

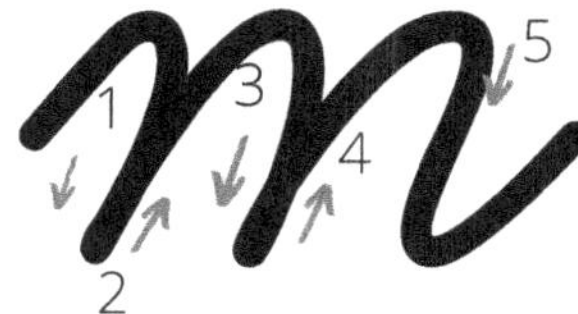

N is for Nickel

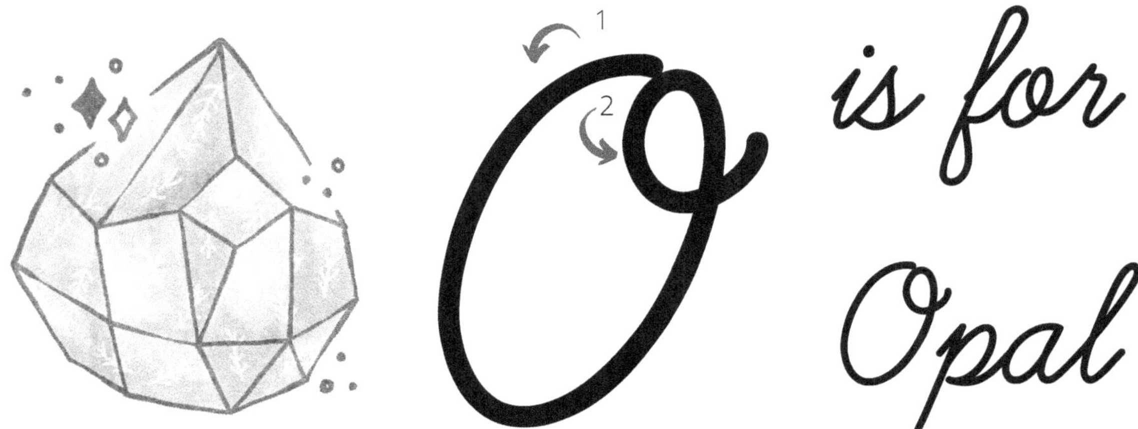

1
2
is for
Opal

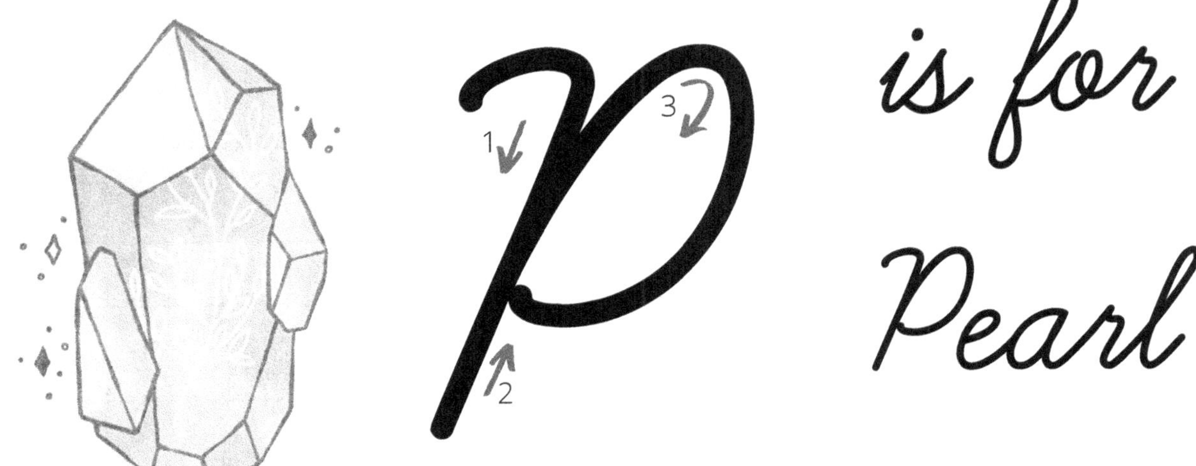

1
2
3
P
is for
Pearl

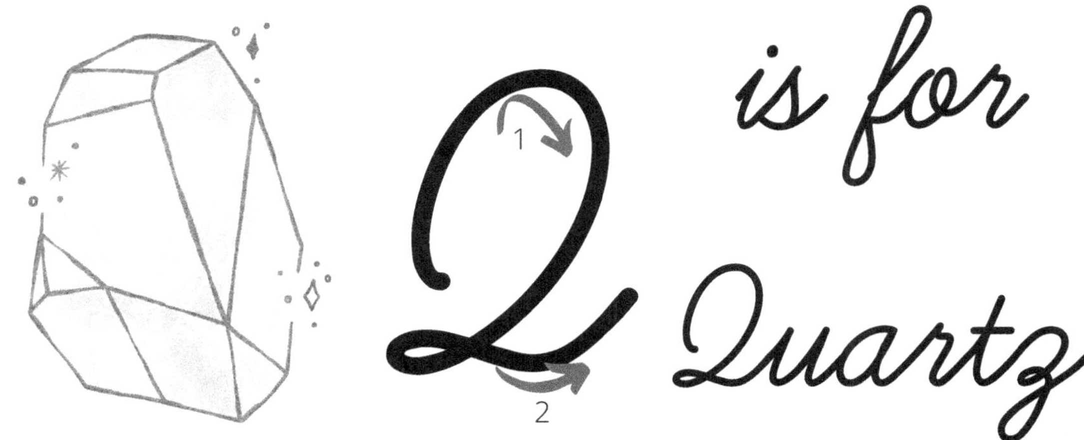

is for
Quartz

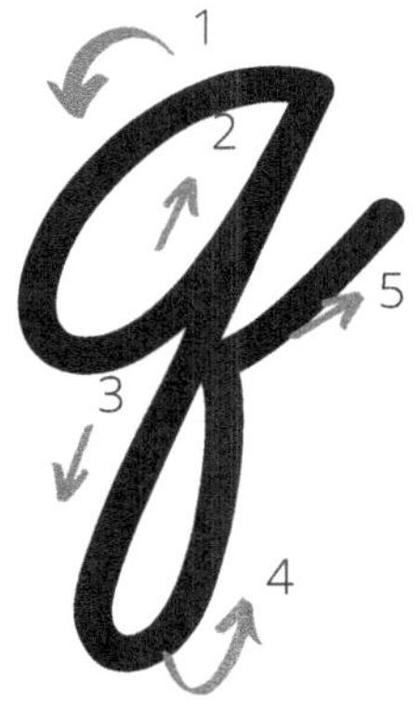

1
2
3
4
is for
Rhodolite

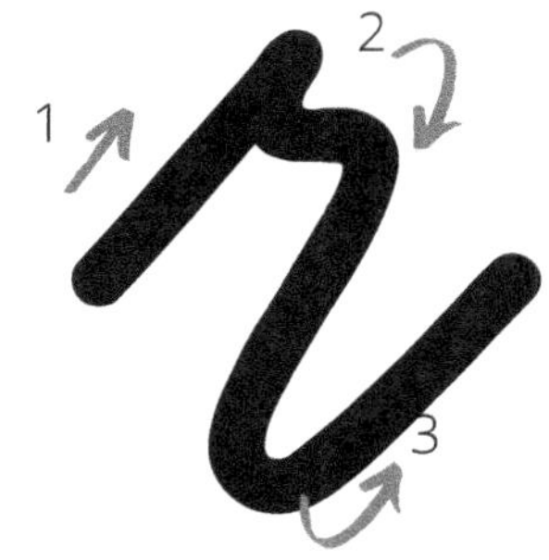

is for
Sapphire

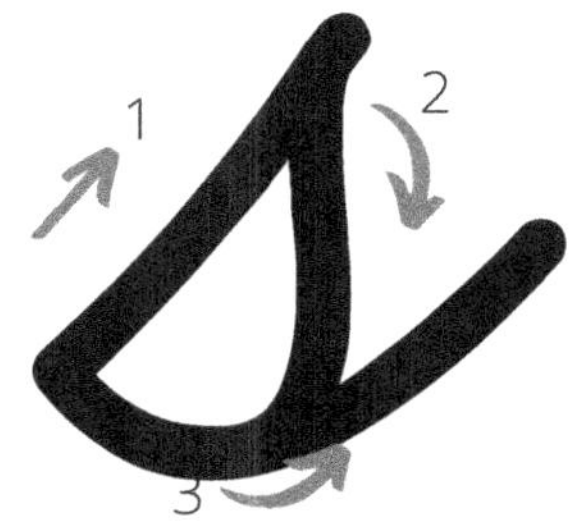

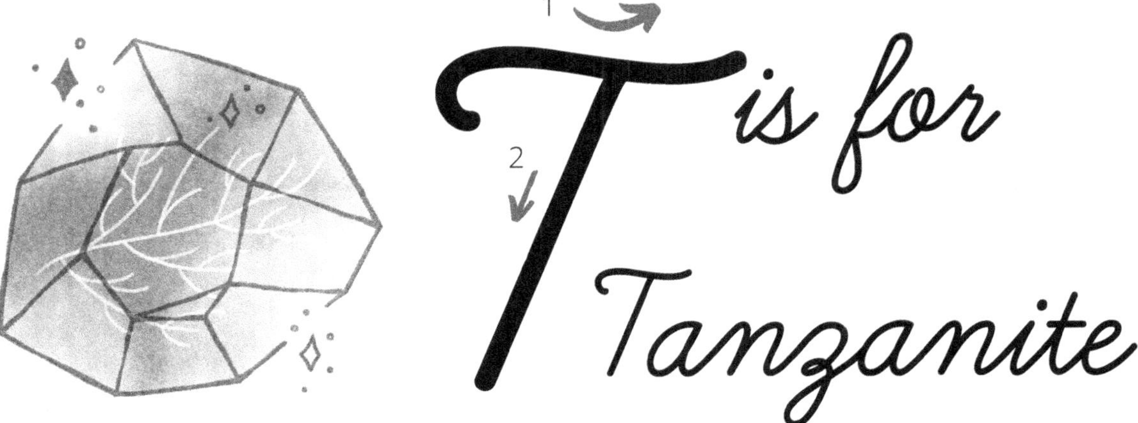

1
2
T is for
Tanzanite

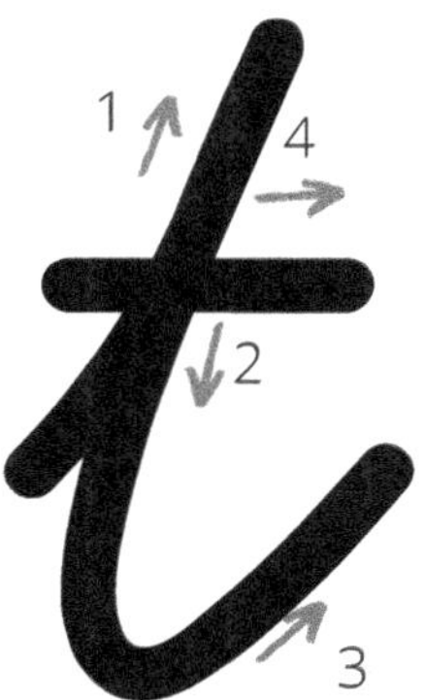

1
4
2
3

1
2
3
is for
Unakite

$\mathcal{V}$ is for Viridine

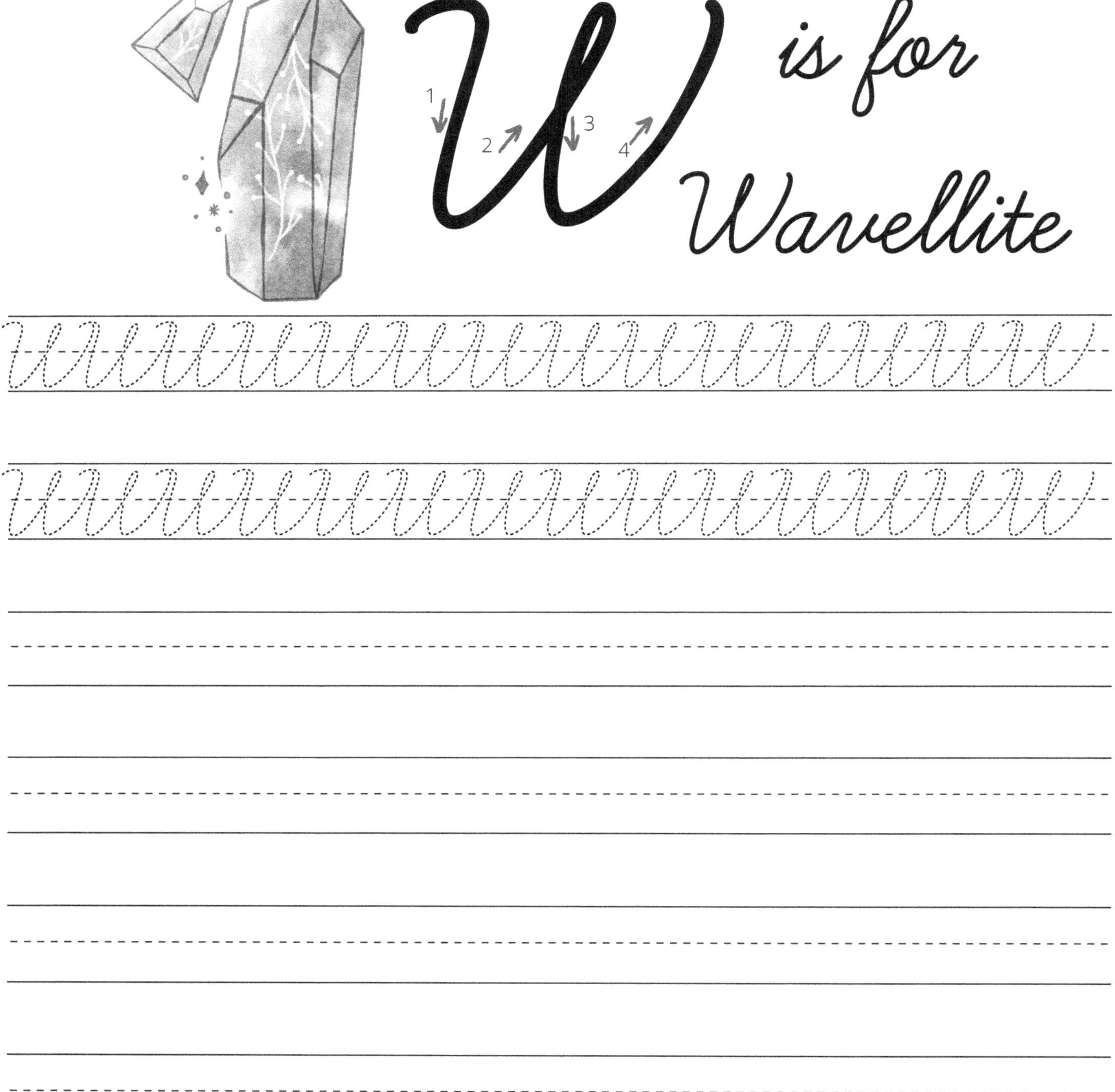

W
is for
Wavellite

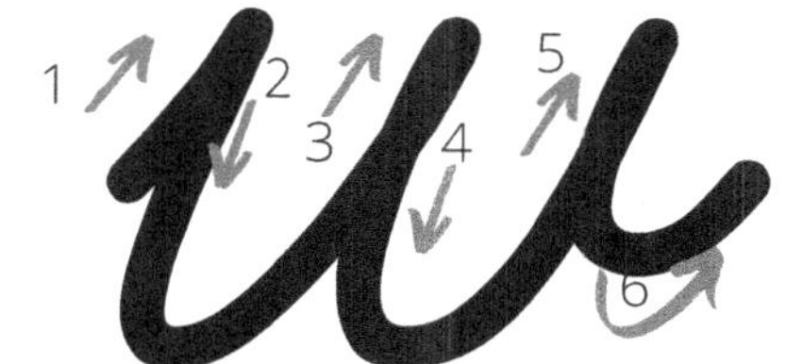

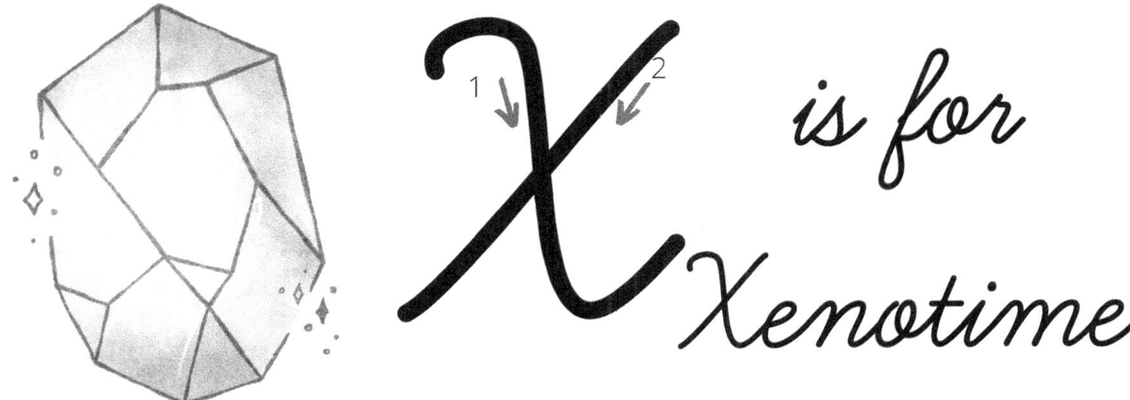

X
is for
Xenotime

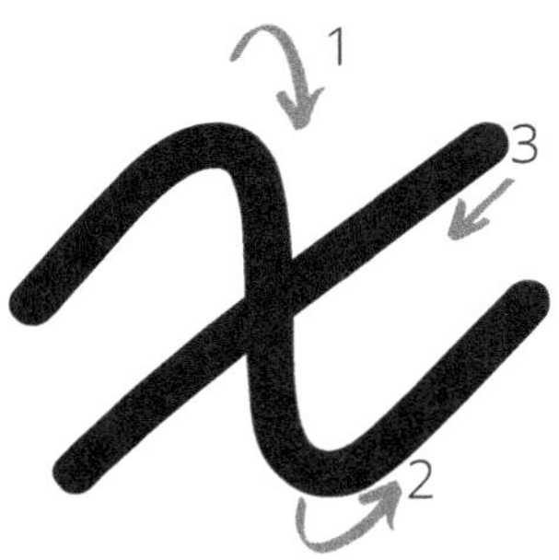

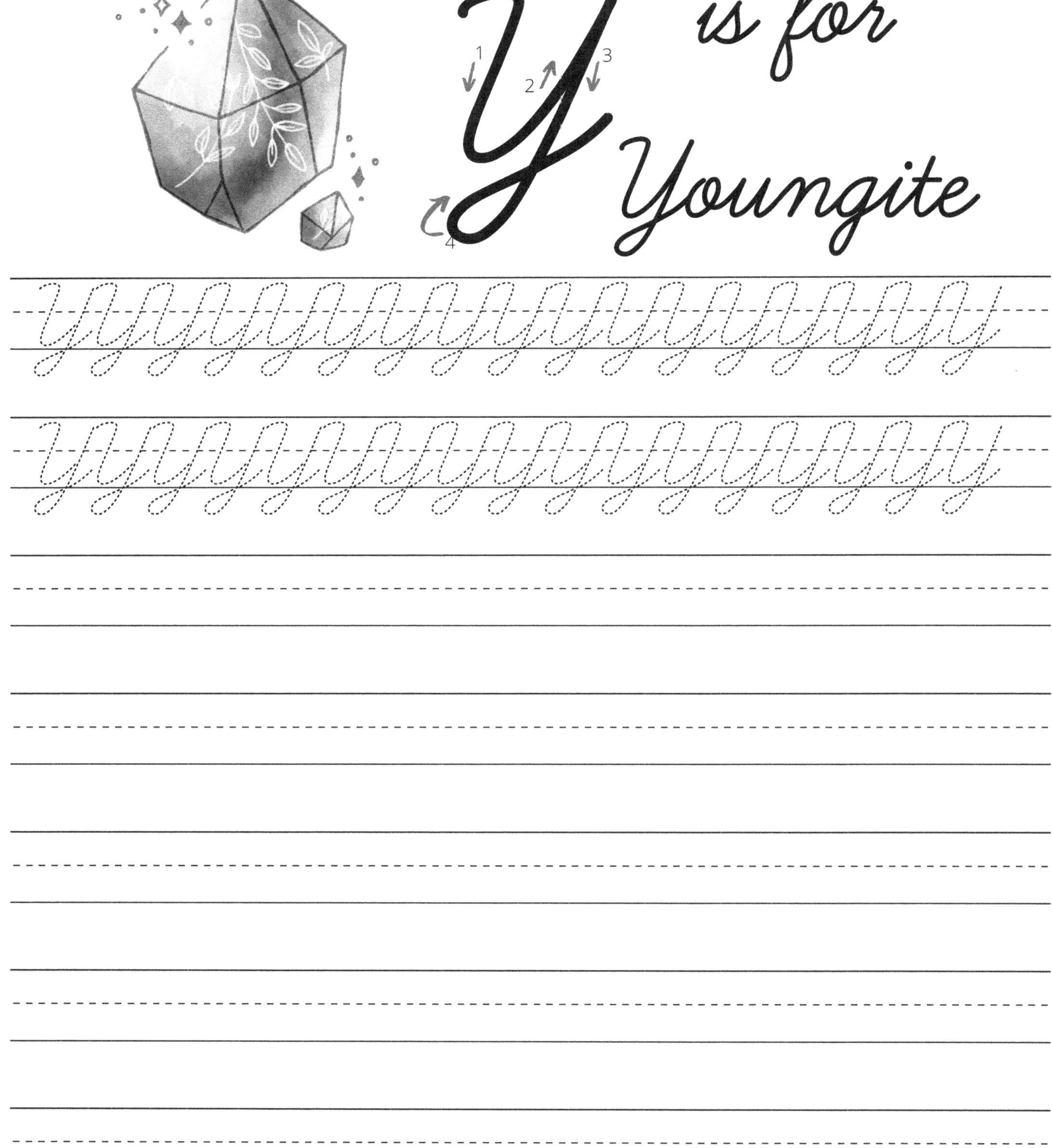

is for
Youngite

is for
Zircon

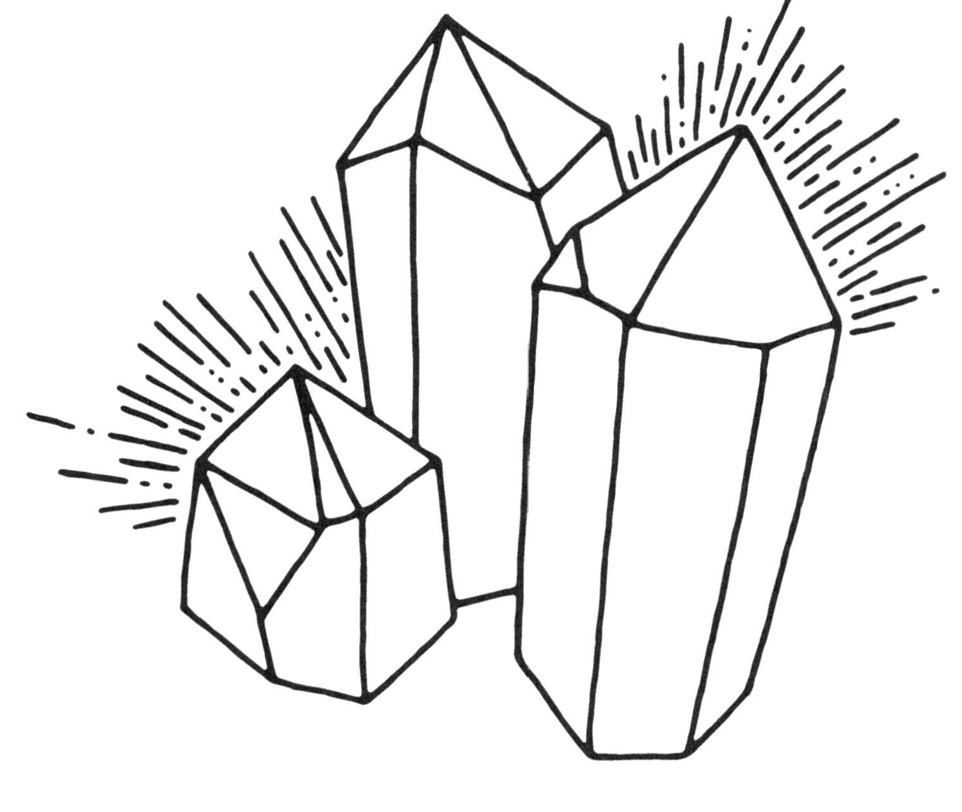

Advanced

Cursive

Practice

Agate minerals have the tendency to form on or within pre-existing rocks, creating difficulties in accurately determining their time of formation. Their host rocks have been dated to have formed as early as the Archean Eon. Agates are most commonly found as nodules within the cavities of volcanic rocks. These cavities are formed from the gases trapped within the liquid volcanic material forming vesicles. Cavities are then filled in with silica-rich fluids from the volcanic material, layers are deposited on the walls of the cavity slowly working their way inwards. The first layer deposited on the cavity walls is commonly known as the priming layer.

The mineral aggregate heliotrope, also known as bloodstone, is a cryptocrystalline mixture of quartz that occurs mostly as jasper (opaque) or sometimes as chalcedony (translucent). The "classic" bloodstone is opaque green jasper with red inclusions of hematite. The red inclusions may resemble spots of blood, hence the name bloodstone. The name heliotrope derives from various ancient notions about the manner in which the mineral reflects light. These are described, e.g., by Pliny the Elder (Nat. Hist. 37.165).

Citrine is a variety of quartz whose color ranges from a pale yellow to brown due to ferric impurities. Natural citrines are rare; most commercial citrines are heat-treated amethysts or smoky quartzes. However, a heat-treated amethyst will have small lines in the crystal, as opposed to a natural citrine's cloudy or smokey appearance. It is nearly impossible to differentiate between cut citrine and yellow topaz visually, but they differ in hardness.

Dichroite is a strongly pleochroic mineral, and its color will be noticeably different when viewed at different angles. It is one of the few minerals that exhibits such strong pleochroism, and is the most well-known mineral displaying this optical property. In its most typical habit, when a transparent Cordierite specimen is viewed through one angle, it will be violet-blue to blue, and when shifted it will turn gray or yellowish.

Emeralds in antiquity were mined in Egypt at locations on Mount Smaragdus since 1500 BCE, and India, and Austria since at least the 14th century CE. The Egyptian mines were exploited on an industrial scale by the Roman and Byzantine Empires, and later by Islamic conquerors. Mining ceased with the discovery of the Colombian deposits; only ruins remain.

In 1852, fluorite gave its name to the phenomenon of fluorescence, which is prominent in fluorites from certain locations, due to certain impurities in the crystal. Fluorite also gave the name to its constitutive element fluorine. Currently, the word "fluorspar" is most commonly used for fluorite as the industrial and chemical commodity, while "fluorite" is used mineralogically and in most other senses.

Garnet species are found in many colours including red, orange, yellow, green, blue, purple, pink, brown, black and colourless, with reddish shades most common. Garnet species' light transmission properties can range from the gemstone-quality transparent specimens to the opaque varieties used for industrial purposes as abrasives. The mineral's luster is categorized as vitreous (glass-like) or resinous (amber-like).

Heliotrope was called "stone of Babylon" by Albertus Magnus and he referred to several magical properties, which were attributed to it from Late Antiquity. Pliny the Elder (1st century) mentioned first that the magicians used it as a stone of invisibility. Damigeron (4th century) wrote about its property to make rain, solar eclipse and its special virtue in divination and preserving health and youth.

As a gemstone, elbaite is a desirable member of the tourmaline group because of the variety and depth of its colours and quality of the crystals. Originally discovered on the island of Elba, Italy in 1913, it has since been found in many parts of the world. In 1994, a major locality was discovered in Canada, at O'Grady Lakes in the Yukon.

During Neolithic times, the key known sources of nephrite jade in China for utilitarian
and ceremonial jade items were the now-depleted deposits in the Ningshao area in the Yangtze
River Delta (Liangzhu culture 3400–2250 BC) and in an area of the Liaoning
province and Inner Mongolia (Hongshan culture 4700–2200 BC). Dushan Jade was being
mined as early as 6000 BC. In the Yin Ruins of the Shang Dynasty (1600 to 1050 BC) in
Anyang, Dushan Jade ornaments were unearthed in the tomb of the Shang kings.

Kunzite is a pink to lilac colored gemstone, a variety of spodumene with the color coming from minor to trace amounts of manganese. Some (but not all) kunzite used for gemstones has been heated to enhance its color. It is also frequently irradiated to enhance the color. Kunzite was discovered in 1902, and was named after George Frederick Kunz, Tiffany & Co's chief jeweler at the time, and a noted mineralogist. It has been found in Brazil, US, Canada, CIS, Mexico, Sweden, Western Australia, Afghanistan and Pakistan.

Lapis lazuli artifacts, dated to 7570 BCE, have been found at Bhirrana, which is the oldest site of Indus Valley Civilisation. Lapis was highly valued by the Indus Valley Civilisation (7570–1900 BCE). Lapis beads have been found at Neolithic burials in Mehrgarh, the Caucasus, and as far away as Mauritania. It was used in the funeral mask of Tutankhamun (1341–1323 BCE).

Pink beryl of fine color and good sizes was first discovered on an island off the coast of Madagascar in 1910. It was also known, with other gemstone minerals, such as tourmaline and kunzite, at Pala, California. In December 1910, the New York Academy of Sciences named the pink variety of beryl "morganite" after financier J. P. Morgan.

Use of nickel (as a natural meteoric nickel–iron alloy) has been traced as far back as 3500 BCE. Nickel was first isolated and classified as a chemical element in 1751 by Axel Fredrik Cronstedt, who initially mistook the ore for a copper mineral, in the cobalt mines of Los, Hälsingland, Sweden. The element's name comes from a mischievous sprite of German miner mythology, Nickel (similar to Old Nick), who personified the fact that copper-nickel ores resisted refinement into copper.

Precious opal shows a variable interplay of internal colors, and though it is a mineraloid, it has an internal structure. At microscopic scales, precious opal is composed of silica spheres some 150 to 300 nm in diameter in a hexagonal or cubic close-packed lattice. It was shown by J. V. Sanders in the mid-1960s that these ordered silica spheres produce the internal colors by causing the interference and diffraction of light passing through the microstructure of the opal.

Pearls are formed inside the shell of certain mollusks as a defense mechanism against a potentially threatening irritant such as a parasite inside the shell, or an attack from outside that injures the mantle tissue. The mollusk creates a pearl sac to seal off the irritation. Pearls are thus the result of an immune response analogous in the human body to the capture of an antigen by a phagocyte (phagocytosis).

While the majority of quartz crystallizes from molten magma, quartz also chemically precipitates from hot hydrothermal veins as gangue, sometimes with ore minerals like gold, silver and copper. Large crystals of quartz are found in magmatic pegmatites. Well-formed crystals may reach several meters in length and weigh hundreds of kilograms.

Rhodolite is a varietal name for rose-pink to red mineral pyrope, a species in the garnet group. It was first described from Cowee Valley, Macon County, North Carolina. The name is derived from the Greek "rhodon" for "rose-like", in common with other pink mineral types (e.g. rhodochrosite, rhodonite). This coloration, and the commonly inclusion-free nature of garnet from this locality, has led to rhodolite being used as a gemstone.

Sapphire and rubies are often found in the same geographical settings, but they generally have different geological formations. For example, both ruby and sapphire are found in Myanmar's Mogok Stone Tract, but the rubies form in marble, while the sapphire forms in granitic pegmatites or corundum syenites.

Tanzanite was formed around 585 million years ago during the mid-Ediacaran Period by massive plate tectonic activity and intense heat in the area that would later become Mount Kilimanjaro. The mineral is located in a relatively complex geological environment. Deposits are typically found in the "hinge" of isoclinal folds.

A good quality unakite is considered a semiprecious stone; it will take a good polish and is often used in jewelry as beads or cabochons and other lapidary work such as eggs, spheres and animal carvings. It is also referred to as epidotized or epidote granite.

Viridine, also known as mangan-andalusite, is a bright green variety of Andalusite, containing iron and manganese. Gemmy rough is small but it can be cut into attractive intense green stones.

Wavellite was first described in 1805 for an occurrence at High Down, Filleigh, Devon, England and named by William Babington in 1805 in honor of Dr. William Wavell (1750–1829), a Devon-based physician, botanist, historian, and naturalist, who brought the mineral to the attention of fellow-mineralogists.

The name xenotime is from the Greek words ΚΕΝΌΣ vain and τῑμή honor, akin to "vainglory". It was coined by French mineralogist François Sulpice Beudant as a rebuke of another scientist, Swedish chemist Jöns Jacob Berzelius, for the latter's premature claim to have found in the mineral a new chemical element (later understood to be previously discovered yttrium). The criticism was blunted, as over time "kenotime" was misread and misprinted "xenotime". Xenotime was first described for an occurrence in Vest-Agder, Norway in 1824.

The classification and naming of jasper varieties presents a challenge. Terms attributed to various well-defined materials includes the geographic locality where it is found, sometimes quite restricted such as "Bruneau" (a canyon) and "Lahontan" (a lake), rivers and even individual mountains; many are fanciful, such as "forest fire" or "rainbow", while others are descriptive, such as "autumn" or "porcelain". A few are designated by the place of origin such as a brown Egyptian or red African.

Zircon is common in the crust of Earth. It occurs as a common accessory mineral in igneous rocks (as primary crystallization products), in metamorphic rocks and as detrital grains in sedimentary rocks. Large zircon crystals are rare. Their average size in granite rocks is about 0.1–0.3 mm, but they can also grow to sizes of several centimeters, especially in mafic pegmatites and carbonatites.

Additional learning resources

A
https://en.wikipedia.org/wiki/Agate
https://www.youtube.com/watch?v=gA2B93OjnmE

B
https://en.wikipedia.org/wiki/Heliotrope_(mineral)
https://www.youtube.com/watch?v=bnpkupLioi4

C
https://en.wikipedia.org/wiki/Quartz#Citrine
https://www.youtube.com/watch?v=D6gtp9ljykE

D
https://www.minerals.net/mineral/cordierite.aspx
Dichroite is another name for cordierite
https://www.youtube.com/watch?v=M1Jx2ST-EVg

E
https://en.wikipedia.org/wiki/Emerald
https://www.youtube.com/watch?v=Gsmv23mYpi4

F
https://en.wikipedia.org/wiki/Fluorite
https://www.youtube.com/watch?v=glGZG1dG0ghs

Additional learning resources

G   https://en.wikipedia.org/wiki/Fluorite
https://www.youtube.com/watch?v=glGG1dG0ghs

H   https://en.wikipedia.org/wiki/Heliotrope_(mineral)
https://www.youtube.com/watch?v=6YXKt0bMBJA

I   https://en.wikipedia.org/wiki/Elbaite
https://www.youtube.com/watch?v=0KXuw6K_VjE

J   https://en.wikipedia.org/wiki/Jade
https://www.youtube.com/watch?v=3Js0cdcKr44

K   https://en.wikipedia.org/wiki/Spodumene#Kunzite
https://www.youtube.com/watch?v=09TdfXrjLJk

L   https://en.wikipedia.org/wiki/Lapis_lazuli
https://www.youtube.com/watch?v=v2JZDdKt3O2

Additional learning resources

m
https://en.wikipedia.org/wiki/Beryl#Morganite
https://www.youtube.com/watch?v=g-13806FYRU

n
https://en.wikipedia.org/wiki/Nickel
https://www.youtube.com/watch?v=btS1rHJclL4

o
https://en.wikipedia.org/wiki/Opal
https://www.youtube.com/watch?v=x9zpWeNW3JU

p
https://en.wikipedia.org/wiki/Pearl
https://www.youtube.com/watch?v=m07OvPEoR6g

q
https://en.wikipedia.org/wiki/Quartz
https://www.youtube.com/watch?v=Nqs3ooCg2yI

r
https://en.wikipedia.org/wiki/Rhodolite
https://www.youtube.com/watch?v=ti2vrnw0du2

Additional learning resources

S
https://en.wikipedia.org/wiki/Sapphire
https://www.youtube.com/watch?v=PL620suV21I

T
https://en.wikipedia.org/wiki/Tanzanite
https://www.youtube.com/watch?v=5TD9z8mPO1c

U
https://en.wikipedia.org/wiki/Unakite
https://www.youtube.com/watch?v=KVOiFX47LE8

V
https://www.gemdat.org/gem-7557.html
https://www.youtube.com/watch?v=uvCsJzOejMU

W
https://en.wikipedia.org/wiki/Wavellite
https://www.youtube.com/watch?v=wVdz5OOnl7E

X
https://en.wikipedia.org/wiki/Xenotime
https://www.youtube.com/watch?v=L21AmrFTr5e4

Additional learning resources

Y
https://en.wikipedia.org/wiki/Jasper
https://www.youtube.com/watch?v=Okmp-qRjymk

Z
https://en.wikipedia.org/wiki/Zircon
https://www.youtube.com/watch?v=V21hFm2P5zM

https://www.crystalvaults.com/crystal-encyclopedia/crystal-guide

https://www.healingcrystals.com/Metaphysical_Directory_Crystal_Guide_Topics_3.html

https://www.minerals.net/

https://www.youtube.com/channel/UC9depPi2ijkug50cDZvIZow

https://www.youtube.com/playlist?list=PLV8P34mamJRJZNAPrq4knuiFcoHMV71-e

Original sources are given with the learning resources for each letter topic.